Womb Mates
Room Mates

Womb Mates
Room Mates

TELA DAWSON

Kravitz & Sons

INNOVATORS IN PUBLISHING, MARKETING AND ADVERTISING

Kravitz and Sons LLC
204 E Arlington Blvd. Suite B
Greenville, NC 27858

Published by Kravitz and Sons LLC.
ISBN: 979-8-89639-763-2 (sc)
ISBN: 979-8-89639-762-5 (e)

To our family and friends who supported and loved us even when they felt left out. To love everlasting and the memories of our twin we carry with us for this lifetime.

And to the creator of all things who paired us with the perfect "womb mate," for just such a time as this.

CONTENTS

FOREWORD

This book is amazing. Once you start reading, you will not want to put it down. It is all true! I have known both of these ladies for many years. They are powered by love. Loss felt, but a reunion one day in heaven. Until that day comes, Tela will continue her time of fellowship and service to the needs of others. These two looked similar, but inside, so different. I hope you enjoy this account of two—so the same, yet so different. Twins: they are so amazing.

Laquetla Hyatt

Tela Mae   Mary Fay
Age three and one-half months

Tela   Mary
Age two years

Tela   Mary
Age two and one-half years

Mary   Tela
Age three and one-half years

Tela Mae, Mary Fay
Age thirty-nine

Mary Fay Petri
Age thirty-nine

Tela Mae Dawson
Age thirty-eight

Mary Fay 1980   Tela Mae
Age thirty-four

Mary Fay Koenig
Clarence Jame Petri
Married May 28, 1966-

Tela Mae Koenig
Gary James Dawson
Married November 19, 1966

Tela
Age twenty

Tela
Age nineteen

Mary
Age nineteen

Mary   Tela
Age six

Tela Mae   Mary Fay
Five years of age
1951

PROLOGUE

A story, a journey, a tutorial of how-tos and how-not-tos.

The unique and very special differences of a precious and very rare gift. Twins. Trails and joys of that gift. Twins.

Love lost and found again. Hope for a future with dreams of porches, tea, and southern hospitality.

To bless and to be blessed. To give more than you take. To leave a mark on this world. One that will rival the memory of monumental women and men that are found in our history books.

Our story, our life, our struggles, and our victories that make up the oneness of twins.

We, the twins of this world, join in one simple voice and call out, "Be yourself, be different, be unique, be proud." Be that voice of the one who was blessed to have been given "a womb mate."

CHAPTER 1

RARE GIFTS

Just like the pages of history are recorded for all generations, we learn from them: all the where's, the why's, and the who's of those that have gone before us.

A story of heroism and those that invented things. And there are hundreds of others who made a name for themselves that will be remembered. These are the people that grace the pages of time in history books.

Our story is not so impressive, but will grace the pages of history for our family.

My history is not finished yet; it is still being written. Chapters and pages of a book that was shared with one so very close. We shared our looks so that very few could not even recognize us or guess who was who.

Like all medical journals and Google-assisted research tells us, all-natural identical twins are rare. Statistics state that three to four births are the norm out of one thousand that are recorded. And fertility drug assists only produce only six to eight births out of one thousand.

Identical twins are rare.

Women are the determining factor because it is the single egg or multiple eggs that are released that will decide if twins or single babies will be born. No matter if there is only one egg or multiple eggs, there are only two types of twins. Identical and fraternal. The other type of twin is called a mirror twin, but this is still the result of the identical twin and when the egg splits.

Men are the makers of boys and girls.

Identical twins share everything, the same DNA; whereas fraternal twins are simple. Two babies born at the same time and share the same birthday. Boy, boy; boy, girl; or girl, girl. Identical twins can never be boy, girl. Why, you ask? Well, because to be identical means mono. Only one egg that divides to make two. The same. Thus the term "identical."

Each fraternal twin has his or her own separate DNA profile.

Identical twins, most would agree are the same, but this is not always the truth. Subtle changes define each of us. We are so uniquely made, and each is created to meet a special purpose in this world. One does not have to look too hard to see this fact is definitely true.

From the time of conception to birth, each little person is being prepared for their special entrance into this world and the role they will play.

Now, as parents, you might aspire for your child or children to follow in your footsteps, or you might be supportive in the new direction they one day will choose. They might choose this new avenue with the assistance of another that is not Mom or Dad. But nonetheless, they succeed.

A special direction for success that will bring each to a clear direction that is ordained by their creator.

This is not a do-or-die directive, but a path of blessings for all who are in or around you.

Blessings for life, love, and more love for us who say yes!

Have you ever wondered now things would be if you did or did not do something?

It is like when a pebble is pitched into a pond or lake. The place where the pebble lands sends forth a ring of ripples that never end until they reach a stopping point. It could be rocks, wood, or the shore.

Our choices are like that pebble that begin a reaction that takes time to reach a stopping point. That point is not for us humans to say, but our choices take a lifetime to reach the end. Why?

Well, we are in life, and this life does not start and stop. It is a never-ending journey until the day our life ends.

To be aware that our choices always bring pros and cons.

To say yes or no could be what directs your ease in life, or the troubles that never seem to end. So think before you leap.

To continue, twins are different in so many ways. Twins that appear to look the same (identical) are because the egg has split. They become the same in every way, even their DNA. That is our gene profile.

However, as an identical twin, I could not be more unique now in my looks and more so in my personality than my identical twin sister.

I am today, like all my yesteryears before. I am more outgoing. A decisive and in-your-face person. My sister, Mary, from birth was quieter and more laid-back. She was always waiting for me to take lead position in almost everything we did.

Momma would always say, "Let Mary go first," and always tell me to "stop putting on the dog." I did not know what that meant. I was just being me.

I asked others about what that means, and I found that the meaning was about being someone different or acting like you are on stage and playing a part that was not you.

The American College Slang of the 1860s. "A flashy display or to cut a swell." Local slang "doggy" was also a popular slang term: attractively costly or fancy. And a more modern is to assume a pretentious air or airs.

Who knew? I must have been practicing for my parts in all the plays I was in later in my years.

Our momma was quieter and more demure too. Maybe I was like my daddy.

People say we have an attraction to those who are opposite. Maybe because we find something in others that seem to be missing in ourselves. Perhaps the feeling that we are complete through them.

Perhaps without really recognizing the connection.

Our daddy gave us nicknames. From the time when we were very, very young, he called us Mary Mouse and Tela Winks.

Mary was very quiet and stayed in the shadows. Ergo the name Mary Mouse. It truly fit her personality—she was always waiting on me to take the lead. Momma was always telling me to let Mary go first, but she did not want to go first—she always told me to go ahead. So I did.

My nickname was a depiction of my personality. "Winks." I was very outgoing and more friendly, more outspoken. My face was smiling, and I laughed a lot. I am still that way today. Life is too short to take everything too seriously. I think that was the first time I really noticed I was different.

I was one inch taller and weighed one pound more. In our lives, that never changed. We married first cousins; they, too, were like night and day.

Mary's hubby, Pete, was a tall drink of water, he stood 6'4. He was quiet in his personality.

Just what the doctor ordered for her. He set her needs perfectly.

I never got the chance to date him, but he was just not my cup of tea. To prove once again our personalities were wired differently.

After only three weeks of dating, they were engaged.

Wow, I was shocked. I really could not see how anyone could have made a lifelong decision in such a short time. Love at first sight, or three weeks. Like I said, "Twins are not the same."

I always knew we sorta looked alike, but we did not come anywhere close in our personalities.

"Cut from a different cloth." I always knew that I was uniquely different, but from what stage in our lives did it become obvious to others? I am not sure. But I kept on being me no matter how many times Momma told me to "be more like Mary."

This concept of being twins, but so different puzzled me. I am made for a special job, and Mary another.

I am, at times, still wondering what my job is, and at others I am clear. Two so alike but made for two separate and distinct jobs.

Each day my plans are made. Checks and balances, yet at the end and completion of a day, I am still at square one. Somewhere in the beginning of said day, my plans are changed. By whom? Well, God did that. And the new day emerges and my plans. Are on point again. A carryover. A do-over I really never considered that my God would make my days, his days. But it happened so many times. But I learned many years ago that I had to rely on him for everything and let him direct his way. Completion and his timing.

Well, we are getting ahead of the story. While we were growing up, our mom was diagnosed with breast cancer. You know that back in the dark days of medicine, that word, cancer—and even today—had a curse with it. A decree of death sooner than later.

We were too young know what that was all about. We were only twelve years of age at that time, but more mature than most of our friends. That is how Mom and Dad raised us. You know, when you are thrown into the water, you sink or swim. And all of our upbringing was about to be put to the test—do-or-die. So we took to the duties of chief cook and bottle washer. Maid and washer woman and chauffeur. All at age twelve, we were driving mom everywhere.

It all seemed natural to us because Mom taught us well: all about the ins and outs of caring for a home.

If we did not take over for Mom, Grandmother—who Mom did not get along with—would come to live with us. For me, it seemed like a great idea. But Mom asked, with tears in her eyes, could we, would we do this for her. Of course, we said yes. Mary and I became all Mom had prepared us for.

I don't think that she ever thought that all teaching would be used so early in our short little lives. Yet Mom was ever so thankful. She had peace of mind and she could begin to heal.

It seemed too real to be real.

We were a household of minors, running life as adults at such an early age. Yet at such an early age we took on that role with ease, all because Mom taught us well.

When Mom came home from the hospital, she needed our help.

Have you ever thought of people who would faint at the sight of blood? I truly never knew it was possible.

We saw blood and stiches—lots of them—and parts of a body without all its parts.

Mom had lost one breast. This was a staggering sight for girls who were just coming of age.

Mary and I were showing our differences again. Mary threw up when Mom showed us her surgical scars. So it became apparent that the changing of dressings would be my job. Perhaps this was a sign of things to come. Our brothers, only eight and nine, were just too young to see such horror, or understand the trauma that their mom was going through.

Mary never got over her fear. "Being butchered"—that is how she viewed Mom and her breast being removed.

Treatments continued, and we drove down town San Antonio with a lot of tears.

All seemed well when one more checkup showed a problem. It was the same over again. What we thought was over was beginning again. It was a horrible time for us, but I cannot imagine

how Mom and Dad felt.

You know all have what some describe as crosses to bear. But we were so young to experience such a heavy cross.

We began to live on the edge. Every time Mom went for treatments or had another doctor appointment, we would ball up in momentary fear, not knowing what might be said. But Mom took it like a strong man might.

Mom said she only had one prayer. Her prayer was to see all her children get old enough to be on their own.

Her prayer was answered. She lived another twelve years. All her children were on their own. God honored her sincere prayer. Only from a mother's heart. She was more concerned for all of us than for herself.

She was only fifty-two when she went to heaven. We all lost the love of our mother forever. Dad was just about fifty-three years old. I think a young man, but he cried like a small child. His wife, his love gone, and he couldn't fit it.

Now we all had to go on. Loss is just that. No one wins. The hole it leaves is not easily filled.

Life does go on, and we all had to move on. No matter the hurt.

Daddy traveled with his job; he met a nice lady. Her name was Alice, just like Mom's. She was petite with dark hair. Very similar to Mom, Dad said, and quite a looker—just like your mom.

I was so very happy. Daddy had a smile again. But that was not to last. At least not with Alice

2. Dad and Alice 2 had begun to talk about marriage. She stopped for a moment. Dad was very concerned. She smiled, and Dad relaxed. The next words that she spoke were an affirmation of her love and then stated, "But first I will have to get a divorce." What? "But I would love to marry you." But! And Daddy took a second breath. I think you have knocked him over with a feather.

I truly don't know if they finished lunch or not, but he said he never stepped foot in that little café ever again. He loved and lost. He always said that Alice 2's husband could still be looking for him.

We laugh about it now. In all it must have scared the living daylight out of him. Like always, time marches on, and Dad is—well, it was my perception—not smiling inside or out.

Daddy visited a lot. That was so great. He would call and ask what's for dinner. I would tell him wieners and sauerkraut. We always laughed, and then he would say, "Be there in fifteen to twenty minutes." Impossible, I thought, because he lived 325 miles away. But ding-dong, and Daddy was at my front door.

Happiness! I loved my daddy so much. I would take him whenever however I could get him.

More months passed by and still months went by and I received my daddy. Time and time again. "What's for dinner?" More and more.

A man so young to be all alone. Still vibrant and handsome as all get out. Broad chested with salt-and-pepper hair, some of which showed up since he was in high school. And just good- looking all over. But then he was my daddy.

Maybe all girls think that way, I don't know, but for me, he was everything. He was very special.

My grandmother called him Eppa. I guess that was a nick name. His real name was Edward Fred. He was known as Ed to so many, or EF.

Mom didn't have a nickname—for us, it was just Mom.

They say time heals all hurt. I guess that is true because the hole in our hearts began to be

covered with the joy of life. For me, the hole still blows cold hurt through it at times. However, my tears don't flow as freely as they once did. There are memories that momentarily capture my attentions that flash by and remind me of love ones lost.

Time moves forward, and Daddy finds love again. Hurrah! It was a time when "What's for dinner?" came calling.

He pulled me aside, and his face changed. No smile, but very serious. No joke about dinner, but you could see there was something of great importance on his mind. Of course, I feared the worst. Then my concern melted away. "What would you think about me getting married again?"

I was so relieved. I asked why the inquiry. He said he met someone. They had been seeing each other for a while—she was a widow.

I had enough composure to ask her name. He wanted my truthful opinion. I was happy for him. And him having someone to share his life and give him back his smile. My honest truth. He was pleased and told me that Mary, my twin sister, was not in favor. We simply looked at life so differently. I knew she would not replace Mom but could help Daddy face his many years ahead of him with love.

Mary just wanted Daddy to keep visiting her and just nag him all to herself—no scaring.

We both looked at everything with the glass half empty or half full. But we rarely saw eye to eye on anything. Two thoughts for two, not one for one. We were created separately for just such a time as this.

She followed my style in house design and décor. So when I shopped for myself, I would buy her one also.

We didn't really know what middle class was, but I guess we fit that mold. Nothing too elaborate. But our aunt Edith, mom's sister, had more. I liked more and more was my chosen thing. More and more, not less. Big and bigger, not little or small. I liked shiny, not dull. My signature took up two lines. Mary's: just one line.

My husband of many years, Gary, told a friend I was going back to school. He asked what I was going to take. Gary said, "How to draw small." That is really me in a nutshell. I do everything big that is me, and I like me. Mary was always dreaming, but small was her choice.

We were good students. Private schools just like our big sister. Incarnate Word and Ursuline Academy San Antonio, Texas.

Mary was a studyholic. Good grades. But she had to really work like a big dog at it. I, on the other hand, just listened in class, took a few notes, and aced all my tests.

One assignment we were given was to copy the style of a particular poet.

Mary, my darling sister, stayed in our room composing her poetry. I, on the other hand, would sprint from our room to the TV room during commercials and do mine.

The next day at school, the teacher was calling on standards to read aloud their compositions. During that time, I took time to perfect my skills. I rewrote several lines. Then it was my turn. I read my poetry aloud. I must say it sounded really professional. Then my teacher asked me what book I copied this poem from. I did not copy anything—it is my work. She didn't believe me. It was not accepted, and I was sent to the principal's office. She told them that I was a plagiarist. I was found not guilty, but it was so humiliating. I have never been sent to the principal's office ever in any grade. I know you can identify with me if you have been unjustly accused.

When you choose poorly, you expect the consequences, but when you are using wisdom, you expect to be treated with respect. This was not the case with this teacher. I was guilty, and that was her story.

I only disobeyed my parents, Mom, one time. I was a good kid, or that is what I thought.

Story later to follow.

Our two brothers, Bud and John, were forever coming up with different ways to land them in the ER—not on purpose, you see, it was purely by accident.

Mom was always on alert.

The boys played hard and long. Spanking for them seemed to always be in fashion. They were handed out on a regular basis.

Mary and I were not as aggressive. No spanking for us.

In our school there were two classes for each grade. Mom placed Mary in one, me in another. We had different teachers, same books, and different homework. We began to develop new friends. However, when you share your lives as twins, you are never known as Mary or Tela. Just the twins. So every party, boy or girl dance, roller rink outing, we were always invited as the twins.

As we began to grow up, we began to develop a desire for unique and different pursuits. When we were noticing boys, we found baseball to be a prime playground for hunting a prince charming. Our brothers played at the same, field so we could see our dream prince. It was all just a hope and a dream because we had not dated yet.

A few years passed by, and our dream prince became real: we got to see them play baseball, a game I understood.

Dances, parties, youth club, and military balls were the perfect place for each of us to show off our individual styles.

Our whole life until eight grade: we dressed alike, wore our hair the same, same shoes, same everything. Even our room we shared since birth was like looking in a mirror again and again. Double curtains, bedspreads, furniture— all the same.

One day, we looked up and rebelled. We moved our room all around. One side was my design, and Mary's— well, it looked just like mine. A mirror image, she copied mine to a tee.

Perhaps it should have been a clue of the things to come. You know interior design. But no, I was happy that she saw a plan she could enjoy.

CHAPTER 2
FOUR EYES TWIN TUNED

The clue to a lifelong pursuit to follow my lead, and one of design for me, "Design by Tela." Dances, parties, and dates: that was the twins. Mary and I wore glasses. We were called four-

eyes and "the twins" until after high school. From first grade on up, it was a handle that simply described us.

The four-eyes nickname seemed to hurt Mary, but me—well, with my aggressive personality and thick skin, I just laughed it off and gave back some smart words to smush their dumb ones.

It was just kids. But for me, myself, and I, it was a great learning tool that has helped in some tough times in life.

I could dish it out as fast as it came toward me.

Bless her heart, Mary seemed to be unsure about so many things. She was always second- guessing her decisions and trying to hatch mine.

As we grew up, our young girl dreams of boys, dates, and clothes changed.

She would set her sights toward boys and young men who were, in my mind, never anyone I would say yes to.

And yet again we began to develop a hunger for different and unique people, places, and things. However, one always has to remember that we, Mary and I shared our everything in life from the beginning. And that bond, I guess, was just stronger than dirt. That desire to protect each other greater than one night imagine.

Point: we were enrolled at a private all-girls school and a dance was planned. Well, it was like a Paul Jones. Girls' choice, so we had to ask a boy to be our date for the dance.

Mary asked a handsome young man she fancied; I did too, so off to our first high school dance. Quite exciting, it would seem. But Mary's date called a few days before the dance cancelled. Something about his grandmother. She stayed home. My dream date picked me up in his mom and dad's big old mobile car. He opened the door for me. I felt like a princess. I felt bad for Mary, but I was not going to make me have a bad time. So off we went.

We arrived at the dance, and it was good. We walked into a gym that was decorate so beautifully. I was a pig's ear turned into a silk purse, and then I glanced forward and my blood began to boil. It was him. That lying dude that had stiffed my little sister to go with another. How could he? Mary was so sincere, and he was lower than a snake's belly. It was clear to me that he would not leave this dance without a piece of mind left on him to reflex his lying dog personality. Whatever it took to defend my twin sister. I crossed the gym floor. I then began a siege against the enemy. A quick battle plan that would wipe out his smile and that of his innocent date.

I was like a mama bear protecting her cub. He had hurt my baby sister. I was there to protect and defend without a drop of blood shed.

Mary was not just my twin sister, but my best friend and womb mate from the beginning. How could I not defend her name, my honor, her honor, her very person with all my might?

This I know. Enraged with my protection mode, I could have slayed a dragon and rescued her from the tall tower like Rapunzel.

My mouth took over, and a harsh warning erupted. "Do not ever call her again after you call her and apologize to her for your despicable character." The next day after the dance he called and his deep regrets were spoken. Plus, he never was heard from again. It worked. I was a force.

I really felt like a big sister. We are only twenty minutes apart in age. But I am still her big sister. And would be that; I would defend her always with the same intensity. A defender of my little sister to protect whenever it was needed.

I do not really know if word got around about me, the twin sister Tela, but it never happened again. I wish I knew if Mary felt the same: "the defender of Tela." But we never discussed that issue.

We were, I guess, just different: strong and outspoken and shy and quiet. One who leads and one who follows.

As we progressed in age, so did our skills in cooking and house cleaning. To this day I still don't like either one. But Mary was on her way to being Little Miss Mary

Housekeeper. She loved it. I only cook now because we want to eat. Simple pimple, easy pizzey. I am not a bad cook—just not a gourmet chef.

Our choices in clothes remain decidedly different. I was bolder in my choices. Mary: more subtle or subdued in here. Bold in color and fabrics—that was me.

Underneath we still possessed a oneness. I guess you could tell we grew up in the same house with the same rules. A mama bear that taught her cubs all of the same survival tricks.

We were so blessed to come into this world with a friend already built in: a womb mate from the beginning and a roommate until we parted ways in marriage. You know, now that I think about it, I have never had a room of my own. I have always shared with my two true loves. Mary and my husband. That's a pretty good gift.

When we were born, we wore little pink and white bracelets so the nurses could tell us apart.

Maybe it helped Mom and Dad too.

I guess we are all born alike in so many ways, but our characteristics develop over time as we mature.

But I think that those little pink and white bracelets might have been the beginning of my fascination with jewelry. One that has followed me all the days of my life. I like all jewelry, but I own them; they do not own me. With or without I am, still flamboyant. I like sparkle! But make no mistake, I can do without them.

Our time in high school was super special. I loved school. All my friends and parties and dances and military balls. It was a means to an end for me. I was not sure what end that might be, but I would keep looking until it showed itself, Mary was not that excited about school. She had several friends and worked hard for her grades.

I still had an interest in cloth design, but I was not sure how to approach the career.

When I was younger, I played with Barbies. I was drawing, designing, and sewing all their outfits. But time moved on, and so did Barbies.

Mary, my love, liked clothes also; for me, it was a passion. So we both tired our hand at design work in school. Sewing and fashion shows. But that dream didn't seem to last for Mary. Me! I was still on point. To be or not to be: that was the question.

Graduation was fast approaching. And we knew, Mom and Dad had set aside money for us for our further education. We were sure hoping it would cover all because it just happened to be the same amount for our older sister, Ida Genell, six years earlier.

Dad was money smart, and it was enough to get Mary into business school, just like our big sister.

My sights were set a bit higher. I entered art school, and Daddy covered all the cost. I was so pleased. I almost thought I would have to use my little savings. But Daddy came through. It, art school, was my happy place. I didn't have to work too hard because it just came naturally.

After a time at art school I was asked to complete a project on a time line. It seemed to be a normal request. But for the first time in school, any school, I felt the pains of pressure to perform on cue. My hands sweat and my head hurt. How could I? I was not inspired. I found really quick that commercial art was not my dream. I felt so disappointed in myself. I didn't know if I would be able to complete anything at any time. Did I disappoint my parents? Of course not! I was Little Miss Winks. So I took another avenue in school. Creative writing. I was a cinch. The stories came so easy. No matter what I was asked to do, I did with ease.

Mary was still in business school and top of her class. She was so good at studies and details.

She was excelling.

It made me so glad we both found something we loved. Yet as before, we were different in what floated our boat.

I guess it takes all types to make this world go around, and we were certainly living proof of that. Two: the same, identical, yet profoundly distinct.

Just before graduation I was asked to interview for a job with a doctor. An OB-GYN lady doctor.

I really didn't know what I was interviewing for, yet as we talked, he gave me several tests to learn how well I listened and how well I thought on my feet. I passed with flying colors. I was hired. He was impressed with my skills and told me so. My ease with people and my basic knowledge of everything. That was what he wanted and needed.

A new door opening for me. Little did I know it was the start of a new career. A new love of medical that was dormant since Mother was diagnosed with cancer. It was calling me, and I wasn't even looking.

Mary worked in an office with books and all secretarial duties.

I embarked on a very new love. The medical field, the people, the excitement all waiting for me. New knowledge of the human form. Biology was one thing in a book, but this was real bodies, real life.

My job started in the front office greeting all the patients, then letter writing, ordering prescriptions, and next, I was helping in the exam rooms.

It was so very easy. I loved it.

Mom took me to work and picked me up every day. She got tired of after six months. I had some money saved up, and Daddy took me car shopping. We went all over and ended up looking at new cars. He always had used cars and said he didn't what me to have car trouble like he did. So I got a new car. My job paid well, and Dad said it was a good investment.

Mary was also working and she, too, was beginning her car search. She only searched for used cars with Daddy. No matter what he said, her mind was made up.

Again, our unique differences showed up. She picked out an older car. It was so ugly in my opinion. But she had her mind made up. I was, in the meantime, pleased as punch with my brand-new car. No problems, but that was not the case with hers. She got it home, and in two weeks it was needing repair. Who knows how much more her used old ugly car cost her in the long run?

Cars, friends, teachers, food, and possible careers were now what each of us would have to make on our own. Just us—no one else. We could not rely on each other anymore. She had to do this on her own. Was I ready to be the sole decider of my own destiny? It didn't matter now because it was all me, no one else, so if it went wrong, I couldn't blame it on her, or her on me. It became a grown-up decision. Mom couldn't tell me to wait on Mary to go first; it was up to her now to sink or swim with her own dreams.

In my generation, all little girls were trained to be housewives and mothers. So it you were going to buck this tradition, it was going to have to be for a good reason.

For a girl that thought boyfriend, dates, and marriage was all there was, she was now beginning to see a possibility of other choices. To go against your generational training was scary. But it was truly intriguing.

Mary and I continued to date. But there was no one that peaked our interest or sang to our hearts. So onward we went. Holiday and parties with the promise all young girls have of her prince charming arriving on that white horse and sweeping her up, up, and away.

But make no mistake about it: we never, never picked the same type of guy.

I never made a list of how my prince would look, but I was drawn to young men with blondish hair color. Mary? The same.

I think our idea of love and Prince Charming and happily ever after came from the movies. Doris Day and Rock Hudson type movies where everybody was handsome and the girl was a beauty. Fall in love, and into the sunset they went.

But movies are not real, so we kept on hunting. And our hopes and dreams were still in play.

Fairy tales, romances: our dream.

When Mary would finally make a choice on anything, she hardly ever changed her mind.

So it took only three weeks for her to make a lifelong choice for a mate, and me: a year and a half. But before that happened, we continued to date. I met loads of medical people. You know, potential doctors and medical researchers. They asked me out, and I felt like Cinderella going to the ball. Which one could be my Prince Charming? A doctor I dreamed about when I was a little girl. Maybe yes, maybe no. Time will tell. I set my plan in motion to snag me a doctor mate. Some took the bait: me, and some passed. I thought, their loss. My now husband said that I set a trap. Not me! I was just my alluring self. I couldn't help it if someone took my bait. But plans don't always work out.

So my plans didn't work to snag a doctor because God had other plans. And so it was. My plans fell by the way side. My trap was full of holes. But I kept trying, hoping to succeed over and over. I was the energizer bunny. I just kept going.

I dated more and more and landed me a good-looking Maraboro man. He was six years my senior. I was not yet twenty, and he was a man of the world. He was interested in me. I felt special. He was handsome, tall, strong, and very polite. My mom's dream for me.

Our big sister Ida Genell met and married an older man also. Mom always said he will know how to care for you.

So who was I to not believe? Mom said yes, but I didn't yet.

He was an x-ray tech. He said he was going back to school and study to be a radiologist. Dr.

Thomas, and I was maybe going to be Mrs. Dr. Thomas.

It was a fairy tale in the making. We were not engaged yet, so I continued to date others.

I was still up for dinner, parties, and movies. Just as many as this little lady could make time for, and the story goes on. More freebies: that was how I rolled.

Mary and I were alike in that way.

All the boys and men we dated paid. That was what Mom and Dad said. No young girl, no matter the reason, would or should ever pay. That was a rule from the handbook of Moms and Dads in the south. Today my rule is still that boys pay. I was a decoration on the arms of my bows. So it was a gift to them. So they had to pay. Ladies are ladies, and we should let men be gentlemen.

Mary dated a lot, but not as much as I did. Perhaps she was pickier. As for me, like I said, movies, parties, dinners: I was out for a fun time. So I tried my best to give all the young men a chance.

Mom always said. "Give them a chance. You don't know if you don't give them a chance." So I was an obedient child. Besides it followed my freebie rule.

I was trawling for men just like a fisherman. I had to put my line out and test the waters. This was a game Mary never played. She either liked a guy or gave him the brush off.

Me: I kept testing the waters.

Men are always on the lookout for the next pretty thing to conquer. Why not me? So I just kept trying for that someone special. Us girls and you guys just approach the game differently. Stalk, set, your sights, and hopefully shoot your Cupid's arrows. And we are setting a trap to capture the heart of our prey. Maybe the love for a lifetime.

It sounds like we are hunting for real. But in all truth, we are all on the hunt for Mr. or Mrs.

Right Love.

The Doris Day Rock Hudson type of fairy-tale romance for life.

If you date enough, you begin to realize that the freebie dinner, parties, and movies are not enough. You want to connect with someone you can share life with, connect, and not just be killing time. Your sight becomes more focused and defined.

Love is now closer than you think. With each new introduction, you hone in on traits and gentleness, the ones that make your heart happy.

I asked myself, is this girl becoming less of a girl and emerging like a butterfly into a woman? Has she begun to bloom like the tight bud reaching the sunlight? She begins the transition of a tight bud into a full flower, and her beauty can be smelled for all to enjoy. A young girl changes into a young woman ready for her prince.

A change she could never imagine.

Mary and I are still enjoying the company of several young men.

We are both in school: Mary in business school, me in art school. Me in art school. We were both concentrating on our new endeavors.

We were both single, and Mom's training to be housewives was still in play. But for now we were footloose and fancy free.

Our big sister was married right after high school. But Mary and I knew we were not ready. Besides, no one we dated was ready either. Just too soon to consider marrying anyone. We had too much more living to do. I was still hunting for Mr. Right, and so was Mary.

The would-be doctor came and went. But my hopes were not dashed.

My Maraboro man asked out, and my heart skipped a beat—it turned to jelly. Handsome and an older man of the world. He was that decoration on my arm. It was a dream come true. We dated for months and talked about marriage. A ring at Christmas. I thought I was happy, but he showed his true colors. Words were exchanged, and Mom's warning came back to me. But I was too smart, or at least I thought so. I went to his apartment, watching TV, and then the gentleman turned into a beast. I was so embarrassed, but I was too scared to call my daddy. I made him take me home—Daddy was super protective of his little girls. So I kept my mouth shut.

To this day I knew that I made the right decision.

Just like the principal's office only took once for me to learn a life lesson. Mom asked me about Dr. Thomas, but I just told her we decided to part ways.

We were not engaged, and no love was lost. Once that ended, I was ready for more freebies.

And Mary was too.

I never have been on a blind date, but a dear friend was desperate. Please, please, please! So I helped my friend, and I went out with her cousin to act as a chaperone. He dates was a ladies' man and she was afraid, but he was cute. We embarked on my first blind date, and little did I know, but Cupid had marked me and shot his arrow. He asked me out again, and I accepted. A love story that has lasted fifty-five years so far.

My blind date was beginning to turn into a life mate.

I was busy at work and art school. I asked my boss, the lady doctor, about my suitor. He was always checking on me and my life because he knew my uncle and felt responsible—somehow just like a dad—for my well-being.

You have to remember that in the 1960s we all took care of each other. More hands on for everybody's well-being. It was just a different time. We seemed to be more family oriented. He was protecting me, and I really liked that overwhelming feeling of love.

I loved my job, even though Mrs. Doctor was no longer in the running.

I must have shown such a great aptitude with Doctor P's patients that he began to talk with me about how he knew I would make a great doctor. I was shocked; I never knew I was smart enough yet he saw something in me that had potential.

The next weeks passed, and more talk of my future to be a doctor! I never considered it was a possibility. I had no confidence in me, but he did. He made me an offer to good to pass up. "I will pay for all your schooling to become a doctor, if you want." But I was still not convinced of my ability.

Then one day my boss offered his two cents worth of opinion. He said, "Take it or leave it." The young man studying geology will be a better match for you. He will take care of you. And our children said "Thanks, Mom," for choosing Dad, the geologist.

I was still not sure of my life's career, but I did care for this guy.

Mary also had her opinion. No was her answer—why? I am not sure, but they never quite saw eye to eye on anything; she really didn't like my geologist.

Mary was quiet and I just was not. We looked so much alike, but once we spoke everyone knew who was who. Our hair was different: mine long, and hers short. Our dress: totally different. It had been that way for years. She was subdued in her color choices and style. Mine more showy and couture. My everything matched. For me, it was the only way.

I vacillated between two career choices. One: a clothes designer, and the other: Dr. Tela. Clothes designed by Miss Tela for the discerning women of means, or Dr. Tela, healer of bodies. Hard choice! I was at a crossroads.

However, Mary was extremely pleased with her life. She was a top-notch secretary.

The possibility of going back to school was—how do you put it—terrifying. But my boss didn't give up. I vacillated back and forth, and I didn't choose either career. Love won out. I didn't know it could be so persistent. Cupid's arrows would not let go. The arrows of love were deep in my heart and would not let go.

Respect, like, and love forever plant a root that never lets go, but grows deep…so that even in the hard times, it can withstand the harsh winds of trouble. And there will be storms that rock your boat and try to uproot even the strongest of oaks.

"Be prepared" is the scout's motto. We just never know when or how strong the winds will blow and try to convince our hearts to give up.

Love is the best and the hardest emotion to tame.

We just can't approach or calculate the outcomes, for without us giving 100% all the time we lose sight of love and find ourselves dealing with hate and unforgiveness.

A friend said to me, "they just wanted their life to be normal without all the drama." My answer: "This is life." It doesn't sound so great if we are in a pinch, but when we realize our life here on earth is all about trials, error, and victories.

Hang on and hang in there. We aren't promised that rose garden. Life comes with thorns; no matter the beauty of the rose and the sweet intoxicating fragrance, the reality is there are thorns that will poke us if we hold to tight onto the stems.

This truly is our life: beauty and thorns. We need to handle love with kid gloves. There is never a battle of the heart won with anger or harsh words. Love is to supposed to cover all. A bit of truth and pure wisdom. Remember that we are under attack. Each time we successfully win this battle, we become more able to face the difficulties of life—another emotion of our head and heart.

If I was smarter in my younger years, I might not have spent a lot of nights hugging the far side of our king-size bed.

Mary and I were both little dickens, and we pretty much always thought we were right. If only I would not stay mad, I would have not gotten some of these wrinkles of worry. Now I don't get as many because I let go of my mad sooner rather than later.

All of Mom's training was about to come full circle: I had let loose of Mr. Maraboro man and got a geologist instead.

I set my trap—well, that's what he said—to win his heart. With hugs and kisses, I won his heart. I remember my med school offer, but my heart won out.

Love is like a seed; it takes time to germinate. And then it has to reach through the soil and up to the sun light to blossom. Gary and I had a lot of time under the soil before we were sunshine bound.

So many bumps along the way, but we were love bound and lifelong. Partners in the making. Mary was dating on and off for the year that Gary and I were dating. Some of her dates lasted just one or two, and other a bit longer. But no love yet. Blind dates must bring a lot of folks together. My big sister, my best friend, me, and maybe my baby sister. It would be a slam dunk if she met her honey that way too.

Mary and I were always up for a freebie, coke, dinners, and movies. Perhaps that was just the sign of the times in 1950s to the 1960s.

Well, I picked her a future and I didn't even know it.

CHAPTER 3

SEEING DOUBLE

And then it happened. Gary's fraternity brother needed a date; Mary got the job. However, she was not impressed with blind date number one.

That night we dressed alike for the first time in years. Everything was the same, even our hair. We were the picture of twindom. We really looked the same in every way. For everyone else's eyes, you could not see any differences.

But my sweetie pie knew who was who. Mary was Miss Flirtations that night. A characteristic she rarely displayed. It sounded more like what I would have done. His frat brothers were so very disappointed in me that Mr. Gary was sent to reign me in. They had this dumb code among themselves. "You stay with the one that brought you." For me it was now not a problem because I loved my geologist, but in the times past I, too, was little Miss Flirtations. If you didn't like them, move on. But I was committed to Mr. P. Charming.

He came to my rescue, and my honor was restored. But was I old enough for a lifelong relationship? It was all pretty new to me: this idea of a lifelong mate. But does anyone ever know if you are ready? Yet all the signs were there. Lots of dates and phone calls that lasted forever. And party lines were in force. We shared with others and many times over, I asked to "get off the line." It was a long time ago, but that was the way of things back in that day.

Looking back on my high school days, I can remember two proposals for marriage and the other that I ended.

People always talk about their lost loves, but not me—I just move on. No regrets or love lost in any of any that courted me. I had my Prince Gary, and that took my heart to a happy place.

Mary had a deep burning fire inside of her that would emerge when she or I was attacked, magma boiling from deep down under, ready to ignite and burn all and anything in her path. The mama bear syndrome. Even though I was twenty minutes older, she protected her big sister, me, like she was the eldest.

When she was hurting, I knew it, and when she was sad, I could feel it. Even though we were young and into our older years, we always had that bond that no one could describe or understand. But that is just what twins have and what they are. One in spirit, one that ages of time and miles never could separate our spirit. We were one from the beginning. We simply had a connection. Single children just don't have the oneness with any of their siblings. We are just so much a part of each other.

So what do we want out of life? A huge question. I am still pondering this question daily. There is only thing that never changes. I need and want to do what God wants me to do. Mary and I both were in agreement on that issue. But we both were then and now always searching for other ways to answer that question onward and upward to the day's new direction.

Mary, my dear twin, was still not attached. Gary's first cousin got a Dear John letter. He was coming home for a three-week leave. He begged Gary to get him someone to hang out with. "Anyone, I just can't be alone." Of course, G thought of my sissy Belle. His cousin was footloose and needed a diversion from an old flame.

Gary and Mr. P's moms were sisters. Gary was my Prince Charming sometimes, and Pete, Mr. P, was not for me, but seemed like they might enjoy each other's company. Maybe a blind date that could be her jam on her jelly roll.

He was 6'4, and Mary just 5' tall. A mutt and Jeff couple. They were a sight to see. They spent all his leave time together. Then it was time for him to go back to his ship. He was in the navy. But guess what! They were engaged. Wow, that was so fast. I couldn't believe it. Engaged.

I was always fast at everything and she was slow, but she passed me like I was standing still. Three weeks I was still underground with our seed of love and slow like molasses. She was so far ahead of me, it made my head spin. I still couldn't believe it. How could anyone make that kind of a decision in such a quick time?

The wedding was on, but I was not included. We had always talked about a double wedding. And now our dream was dead—it went up in smoke. I felt so alone, but Gary and I were not there yet.

They married and now I was one—no more roommate. Maybe we would never be together again. It was a road I was not prepared for. She moved to California, and I was still Texas-bound. Gary was still in college, and I was working. We talked about marriage, but not right away.

That would have to do because my double wedding plan had passed me by. I was happy for her, but I still felt left out in left field. But on that day, her wedding day, she was first—it was her day. I was not the center of attention, and that was okay. Her special day. Her moment to shine in the sun. Something she probably wanted to be first her whole life, but didn't know how to get there. Well, she was certainly first that day.

She looked amazing, beautiful, radiant. A gorgeous wedding gown made of French Chantilly lace. Long sleeves, hoopskirt, and beautiful veil of her design.

We were not two anymore—just ones. My dearest confidant was gone; Gary was a man and he just didn't and couldn't understand. Even my best girlfriend didn't get it. Our twindom was for us alone.

Back in the day, Hugh Church had a wedding in vogue. May was her wedding month, and my upcoming was to be late November.

Gary and I had set a date six months after my twin sister's.

Mom and Dad had spent a fortune on Mary's wedding just six months prior. So of course I thought it was my responsibility to help out. I never considered like the brides of today, getting my own wedding gown. We were the same size, so I walked down the aisle with the same French lace gown. My veil was different like me, and that is how I helped out: feathers and toil and lace. Classic and unique all wrapped into one gorgeous veil. It was me.

I was so very afraid of making a mistake. This was supposed to be for life. My heart said yes, but my head was confused. Again, Mom and Dad had spent a lot: 450 guests. If I backed out! I went through my mind and decided on word was the plan.

I said "I do." It felt right, but the insecurities were there. Come find out, Gary had those feelings also. As we followed our hearts our heads couldn't rule us anymore. We are married now and life seemed great.

Mary had moved back to Texas, and it seemed like there were two of us again. I felt so complete. Not too many months passed, and we were separated once again. It would be years before we shared a hometown together.

Mary had lived in California, San Antonio, Dallas, and Houston, for almost twenty years before we reunited. Midland, Texas. Gary and I only lived in two towns. We were still drilling wells in the oil business and me: home design and interior design. It was my passion, so my art school paid off.

A God-given gift that I explore regularly. Mary got to move and move and move again. Those new towns, friends, and new churches, new everything. I was jealous. I wanted to move and have a new adventure. It was my plan, but not what God wanted. We have hoped and prayed, yet we never got transferred. Here for the long fifty years plus. Each day opens new adventures—I just have to take the time to see them.

Mary and I have shared so much over the years, but none so precious as when we shared our birthdays. Once again, we celebrated together.

We both had likes and dislikes. Moose and Winks together again.

We both had joy and moments of pain—children to share. I had two girls and two boys. Mary had two girls (natural) and two precious boys that were adopted. She would always say now we are the same. I never kept score on anything, but she must have. It meant a lot for her to be the same. We shared almost everything. Schools for our children and church where we worshipped.

Mary and I attended private schools. We all wore uniforms. We were famous: "the twins." Everyone knew who we were. You see, there weren't very many twins around in those years. The whole school looked the same: uniforms.

On the days when uniforms were not needed, we got the school to wear civilian clothes. That is what we called street clothes. Mom sewed, and we were always dressed in the latest fashion. She had learned how to sew at a young age. And our shoes were the best leather Italian shoes money could buy.

Mom came from a family of twelve children where there many hand-me-downs and shoes were not accepted. So she wore shoes that did not conform to her petite feet. She swore that her children would never wear hand-me-down shoes, and we never did.

Mom taught us sewing skills that might be used in our future: cooking and keeping house—all skills for our future.

We were different when it came to raising our children.

I was a pretty hard disciplinarian. Mary was letting her children rule the roost.

When I spoke, the children were expected to obey. There was option. Now was my command. Today my children will quote, "The wrath of Mom." A similar quote from the Star Trek Movie. "The wrath of Kahn." I truly didn't know I came across that way, but I had no tolerance for disobedience.

Mary was much more tolerant. Her children would allow Mom to request many times before they would respond. The magma lava was boiling from within her, and then volcano Mary would erupt. Not a pretty sight.

The wrath of Mom brought forth immediate results, and I did not have to raise my voice.

When blue jeans became fashionable, the designer put their names on the front and back pockets of their jeans. They were expensive: one pair of those jeans or more pairs of the Levi's or Wrangler? Mary allowed her girls to choose. One pair. I made the choose for my girls. I was the momma, and my decision stood.

No matter the decisions in life that were made, I am very proud of how our girls turned out.

Mary and I were so much the same, but so different from the beginning. We didn't like the same foods, the same toys, and the same clothes. Even though were dressed alike, we both liked different colors, shoes, books, friends, and sports. We both excelled in cheerleading. It was so important to Mary. I took a backseat to her want and let Mary represent our school teams. I was number two, but I didn't mind. My potential glory was put on hold to let Mary's dream come true.

That is what love is. You give and then give again.

This was a defining moment in our future. Learning how to make someone more important than yourself.

I tried everything in school. One of my loves was theater. Many was there also. I was on stage, and she was behind the curtains. So we both did theater. In each production we took our chosen places.

I never aspired to Hollywood or Broadway, but I had a special talent. And I used that to woo my suitors.

These talents of stage and design were all dangled in front of me. Then medical. Could you see me? Dr. Tela! No, my focus was on my geologist. My Prince Charming: marriage and family. All of my mom's training was coming full circle. Gary had captured my heart.

"And we lived happily ever after," the end of a fairy tale.

Mary and I shared so much. Mom and our grandmother, two of the most fabulous women in our lives, were gone. And love lost was our first experience with such loss: death.

Life does go on, and we did, but a memory that Mary carried was the one of Mom's cancer.

Such trauma and scars. You can't unsee. It enveloped her.

My Mary, my twin sister, my other half was now facing her own tragedy. But you can face a problem and run, and she did. She postponed her checkups for months and more months. fear grabbed her so hard. She was paralyzed. I knew the signs, but no suggestion, no pleading changed her mind. Volcano Mary was ready to blow, so I had to back off. Butchered was the word Mary would use to describe mom's ordeal. She continued postponing her appointments.

Our personalities, loud and quiet, could be seen clearly.

If the truth be told, I wanted to hit her, shake her, and spank her; she was stubborn as a mule. So don't get in her way—you might get kicked. Her eyes were responding to the fire that was boiling deep within her. I could do nothing. I begged, but it didn't move her. I could do nothing. I begged, but it didn't move her. It was as if she was frozen in the concrete of fear; no one was able to reach her—not even her tall drink of water.

Two years passed, and she agreed to go to a Christian Hospital where they would pray and then approach the problem.

That time came and the news was given. She had waited too long. The cancer was all over the tissue. She was captured and became deaf to the plea of all.

Then she faced the disfigurement of losing both of her breasts: bilateral mastectomy. Now we hoped the healing could begin. And a hope for life on our lips in prayer.

Two years passed, and her life seemed to be slipping away. My twin, my womb mate, my best friend was going to leave me never to return, and I couldn't do anything. No procedure, no stem cell, no bone marrow, no blood transfusion. There was nothing I could do. I was helpless. I was faced with the reality of death and life. We had held each other when Mom and Grandma died. Now I would have no one like her to grieve with; our stories and memories together would not be shared again.

I was truly blessed to have had her for that part of my life. A celebration of the memories we shared.

I wanted to ask why was it her time, but I know God has a time for all of us to be born and a time to die. That is my only answer I can accept. Now I count the days and memories I did have with her, and not the days I didn't.

I think of tea and porches and the time we will never have, and then I thank God for everything I did have; grey hair, rocking chairs, and tons of stories we won't have, and my tears begin to flow with thanksgiving. I had more than some people ever get. My dream lost, but life gives me more chances to share them with all, make memories for others to remember; here today and gone tomorrow, but our memories live on in our hearts. Enjoy the trips down memory lane. Don't be afraid and cry—God will help you get through it all.

My memories of my twin sister, my womb mate, and roommate all to enhance my life forever more.

We were identical twins—natural, not drug assisted. Fertility drugs had not even been invented, yet we were a rare phenomenon.

Mary studied very hard, and all I did was cram and take notes. We were good students. We both passed with flying colors—just did it differently first, but she just didn't want to. So I went ahead all the time.

We both wore glasses. A new pair each year, and we looked cute. I thought so. We looked so alike.

We learned to drive at age eleven and became Mom's chauffer during her cancer treatments.

We were very detailed. We just had to be because God knew we were going to need it; Mom depended on us. So did Daddy.

Mary loved to cook—I could take it or leave it. Later in life I had to cook to eat. My motto: simple pimple, easy-peasy. Too much time and too many ingredients made me uncomfortable. I attacked receipts like a mighty warrior.

We were simple and complex. Me: I was organized chaos; Mary was all calculating, Mary made lists for everything. I just let it—everything—happen. We were stunning. We were Texas ladies and we tried our hardest. We took every opportunity to impress and take those pig's ears and transformed them into the silk purse: that was Mom's saying for anything that was ugly, and now if given time, you can change the world.

Mom grew up on a farm and had twelve brothers and sisters. Remember her song. New shoes for all my children. No other hooves in their shoes: another country saying. She didn't talk much of her upbringing, but it had to have been hard.

Three girls and two boys. That was our family. It was good. We only have one chance to love our family. Don't lose the opportunity.

One of my brothers didn't like me too much; a lifelong mate is more like it. That siege never ended until I told him I loved him no matter what because he was my brother. It started when we were very young. He hit, I hit, I ran, he chased. Fury ran after me. Fire breathing from his little nostrils. I got to Dad's workshop, locked the door, and waited until the fiery dragon left. It seemed like an eternity. A place to sit and wait and wait. He left, and I could unlock my tower of safety. All of that time of hate, and all it took was me to love him out loud. He melted, and no harsh words were ever exchanged again. Love conquered his hate. Now the fire can only be found in fireplaces and campfires.

Mary had some of that pent-up fury as well. She would rumble and blow when you least expected. I had, then and now, an intolerance for stupid and I continue our quest for good.

Twindom: are we the same or different? The request for obedience, and we both handled it differently. Mary was quiet and then turned into volcano Mary. Nobody would respond, then she blew. Me: I was the wrath of Mom. I spoke and I required an immediate response. It worked for me.

We were just unique in our approach to this subject.

Miles separated us for many years. Yet our twin connection had had no distance meter. Our phone bills were outrageous. The age of Ma Bell landlines were all we had. No cell phones yet. Our husbands tried to limit our phone calls to once a week. But it didn't work. We tried writing, but our postman had trouble with our letters. They always needed more postage. More like books than letters. We must have paid for Ma Bell's new building and all their employees' salaries. We needed our voices to answer our questions. Letters took long.

Now our cell phones allow a closeness we never could achieve with Ma Bell. Miles apart: use your cell phone and say hello.

Every day, I miss Mary. Every day I used to ask the Lord why was her time up, and not mine; my answer was no answer. All I knew is that my job must not be finished, Mary's job was over, and I had a hard time accepting that I missed her so desperately. It was a really big pill for me to swallow. But this was life. A time to be born and a time to die.

I was told after Mary died that I was to get my affairs in order—why? I was an identical twin with the same DNA profile. Genes. But God did a miracle in me.

I am seventy-five, and Mary was forty-three when she died. It has been many years, and my genes, my DNA have been proven that I did not carry the BRCA gene. Mother and Mary both carried that gene—how else could you explain the miracle except God did do a miracle in me?

According to all medical testimonies, I had three years at the max before I would meet Mary in heaven.

But God is good, and all the time God is good. To this day I have had no cancer anywhere in my body. My job is not finished yet, and prayer does change things.

I try to face all my fears head on. But I still get scared. We are, after all, just human. I face happiness, sadness, joy, and fear just as we humans do, and sometimes it gets the better of me— fear, that is. I have to trust God each day to be my everything, kick fear, when it arises, in the butt, and command it to leave in Jesus's name.

Fear wants to plant a seed deep within us and feeds its roots with everyday problems and disappointments. Don't let the sun go down on your wrath or fear—deal with those attacks of fear and don't let it grow roots.

Mary and I were different in that way—salt and pepper. We complimented each other, but our looks and personalities were as diverse as salt and pepper. Apart these are great, but together phenomenal.

Mary was quiet and approached everything differently. She was always second when I was around. Well, that was her thoughts—not mine.

She was jealous. That was what a friend said she said to her. We never talked of her jealousy.

It wasn't until after death that I became aware of her hurt. We shared so much.

No matter if I was first or second, she was my dearest friend: Mary, my friend since birth.

After Mary went to heaven, I met one of Mary's friends. She was more like me than Mary was; we became fast friends. She made me laugh, and I her. I called her Weezer and I was Clairee. These were names from one of our favorite movies, Steel Magnolias. These two were lifelong friends. They loved each other more than their luggage.

Mary and I share parents and siblings, but Weezer and I were forever friends and soul mates. We were brought together by the hand of God; we cried when Mary died and laughed about stories of Mary's upbringing. Another sister for me from another mother. If Mary was still alive, we three would be the three musketeers.

In my dreams, I always saw Mary and I growing old together, sipping on iced tea, and sharing stories, but that was no more.

CHAPTER 4
STRUGGLES TO BE ONE

Weezer and I were like peas and carrots—we just were meant to go together. And my new twin sister was born, and my heart rejoiced.

I looked at each day as a gift. I giggled again and smiled again. The sun was shining on me and my new twin sister. God knew I needed a new sister; she grew so sweet like that of a newly blossoming flower.

Mary and I were leaders and follower. But we are all equipped for greatness just at different times of life.

We are all part of the body of Christ, and one should desire to be a head if it is not your time for greatness. For without each other to support us, we will fall. Be happy to lead or follow. You will have your day in the sunshine. Maybe it will be on you for a lifetime or just a short time, but nonetheless, God will have his way. Wait and he will bless you.

Encourage, help others in need, and pray. Prayer goes everywhere and blesses the receiver. Mary had one special friend; I had many. I had many dates, and she had less. She was pickier. I was Miss Social Butterfly. She studied hard; I didn't. We had scholarships and excelled.

I was ready for adventures. She was scared; I am flamboyant. Mary was subdued; I was a little wind and crazy. Mary was more guarded. This all boiled down to she and I were two separate individuals. Just like mirror twins part their hair on different sides, Mary and I were the same, yet so uniquely different in almost all we did.

But our desire to protect and defend each other was identical.

We had a bond that could not be explained. Mom told us that we had a language that only the other could understand.

After studying about other twins, this speech thing was a common denominator among all. We probably talked to each other as womb mates.

No one could understand us, but we understood everything the other said. If we didn't speak, our eyes told the story.

She needed me, and I needed her. Our minds set on one another when we were young. After all, we were twins created for a special purpose. We were a gift to our parents. And in time, we learned how to be a gift to others as well.

We leave a mark for a lifetime on our family and friends.

We can be happy and have lots of chances for stardom. Be yourself—you are super special. So if you fail, stop for a moment and get back up on the horse of yours. Use your mistakes to show you can learn and come out the winner. Go forward—it's not that hard.

I asked my children about their aunt Mary and what they remembered. They all said the same thing. "Wait until your father comes home." Mary was laid-back and very comfortable for her hubby to dish out the punishments. Me? There was no waiting for anything. It was right now. Not wait! I couldn't wait; it put too much pressure on me and my husband.

When Gary grew up, those words wait were a torment for him. And then his daddy had to use his free family time punishing all his children. That was definitely not what he wanted to do with his children, and I fit his dream: I took care of business right away. Do the crime, do the time. "The wrath of Mom?"

I love my children, and I would do anything to help them be the fabulous adults they turned out to be. Hugs and kisses, respect, and a desire to honor all no matter where they are in life. We are raising the next generations of the world. We will all reach our destiny in time. It can be easier or more difficult.

You are the parent—be one.

I know we did it differently, but our kids are all great adults.

I was always blessed by my Sissy Belle, and I thank God for my twin sister.

Mary and I had namesakes. Mary was more submissive in her ways; I thought that Jesus's mother must have been like that. Me, I was named after my grandmother. Not her real name, but her nickname. She was a survivor; her husband died early in their marriage with a young child to raise. In the early 1900s, that was truly a trail all of its own.

I was so glad they didn't give me her given name, "Otlilia Amalia." A huge handle to carry— Tela is much better. Thanks, Mom and Dad, for choosing wisely. It is unusual, so I answer to everybody's slurred attempts.

We all have ups and downs, but we can overcome. It just might take time; keep trying.

My sister from another mother, Weezer Boudreaux, is now one I share my hopes and dreams with. We are closer than blood in so many ways. We shed tears over Mary and her memory and excited tears for our new adventures.

Our hair, silver now, and a few worry wrinkles grace our faces. I have almost as much time with Weezer as I had with my Sissy Belle Mary Mouse. I try to take every day and search out opportunity one at a time because we never know when our number is up.

Life is a story to be loved and told. Live it—don't let it pass you by.

When Mary visited, she would rest in the afternoon. As she lay there resting, my little person Chuck went up to her, he called my name, Momma, and she opened her eyes. He blurted out, "You not my momma." My sister laughed, and then it happened. He curled his little fingers together and landed a hit right on her cheek. She was in shock.

But it proves a point: we, Mary and I are different, so much so a two-year-old can tell the difference.

We laugh about that story, and I continue to know that I know we are unique and special and made for just a moment like this: truth that we all know within.

Time marched on, and Mary moved to my city. I was so excited; a party was planned, a kid in a candy shop. What could be more perfect? I could talk and walk and cook now with my Sissy Belle. Could life be more fantastic?

My dream of ice tea, porches, and grey hair. All could come true.

But she was hiding a secret. Fear rose up and the memories of Mom's ordeal covered her. She avoided the mirror, so she didn't have to face the possibility of Mom's end. The mirror told her what she wouldn't acknowledge.

Days passed and my pleas fell on deaf ears; I knew she was facing a problem, but she wouldn't listen to me or her hubby. Two years passed by now my twin was gone.

I was a single child. It was not all I thought it would be; my tears, they had trouble stopping. I went to get our daily 7-Eleven Big Gulp and I only got one. I drove around to the places she liked to go, but it had no happiness for me. I stopped and I was still picking up two camps, two pictures, or two bed covers. You see, that was my joy to bless her because she liked what I liked. One for me and one for Mary. Everywhere I went we had been there: pain I had to overcome.

I try the old places and have new places to visit with my new twin, Weezer.

I miss my Mary. My memories now bring a smile where once a bucket of tears filled my hankies. The holes in my heart, those of loved ones lost, have been filling in with joy and my Weezer.

Mary was satin and lace. I was the same, but sequins, sparkle, and bling were always added.

Elegance in two different ways. We both were that way our whole life. Bling suited me. Mary's hubby liked her just like she was. My geologist loved me and my showy way.

Mary and I both learned how to receive. There was a time we both had more and less, and less is a sickly feeling. It is so easy to buy, bless others, and complete another to receive when you don't have. The moral of this story is: receive with a thankful heart and pray one day you can repay the kindnesses that were shown you.

Mary and I wore glasses growing up. We were called four-eyes. Mary was serious, and it hurt her feelings. I just sounded off at my name-callers. It became a game of wits. All the better to see you with, and the word games continued.

We were just two very different girls. I think it might be the same today if someone dared to be calling us names. As the old saying goes, "A leopard does not change its spots."

When we growing up, our big sister got married. We were junior bridesmaids; Mary was to go down the aisle first. She was twenty minutes younger, so she was the youngest, so first was her pace. A beautiful dress and a huge party was planned after the ceremony.

Rehearsal dinner and the plan was in place. The big day was upon us, and the time had come: sunshine outside and Mary's nerves got the best of her. Hives and big red welts covered her body. She was so afraid.

Moral of this story: nerves make for ugly marks.

I went first, and found it to be loads of fun. After the wedding and her nerves settled down, the big red welts began to subside, and we ate loads of cake and wedding foods.

Mary was afraid; I wasn't. This concern she displayed then was ever present until she died.

Two very unique little girls.

I wanted to be first, and Mary wanted to be second-in-command. To follow and not lead, I was cut from a different cloth.

Mom was like Mary—quiet. But Mom could run a household without raising her voice.

Big sister Ida Genell, Mary, and I all had great singing voices. It was our passion until it wasn't and we all turned our focus, our passion to something else.

I didn't know that one could lose a passion, but we did.

I was always ready to conquer and move on—a new direction, a new passion. Mary stayed the course a lot longer than I ever did.

It just seemed that I was unsettled. I do and then move on. I must be a gypsy at heart: I dream, I plan. I accomplish, and then onto another challenge.

Mary was a quiet friend to all. I was opinionated and tried to change the world.

Mary would make lists, and I just let things play out. And they always did. I now make lists so I can get everything done.

I love all our new gadgets. It makes life so much easier.

We are all programmed to love, and we spend a lifetime seeking it. Mary and I were no different. We tried to win favor with our parents and teachers. It was truly a natural condition. We were always wanting each other's praise.

We were so blessed to have each other, but we were born to do different jobs.

No matter how many miles separated us, we still were as close as the air you breathe. We felt each other's pain and joy.

My twin was gone way too soon. I was born to be a twin and share my first beginnings. Now I want to teach others to understand and accept that we are all different. We were born on the same day. All expected us to be the same, but our personalities, as they developed, were as different as night and day.

I couldn't do her job, and she couldn't do mine.

So let your twins or your twin be unique and special. Be happy to be you.

CHAPTER 5
ME AND ME

As a twin, I have had many experiences. I had a womb mate, a friend, a special opportunity to be closer than some husbands and wives, and loads of memories of someone so very special. Mary Fay Koenig Petri, my twin, womb mate, friend, and confidant.

I will climb the mountain and forge the seas until it is my time to join my sister in heaven.

We should never say at the end of life, "I wish I could have." If we follow our destiny, our bucket list will be complete, and God will say, "Well done, good and faithful servant."

Live, laugh, love, and you will be complete. Bless all you know and all you meet and show others you are the best Christian that they know.

TYPES OF TWINS

From the beginning of time, I have been a twin. No matter how things have or would have unfolded, I knew a closeness, a friend, and love that only twins can know and experience. Our lives can change many times, but the oneness of womb mates will always be the same. You may seek and desire to be you, only you, but to be two is the greatest gift you will receive.

Conjoined twins are two babies who are born physically connected to each other. Conjoined twins develop when an early embryo only partially separate to form two individuals.

Fraternal twin are also dizygotic twins. They are the result when two eggs are fertilized during the same pregnancy, resulting in two of the same sex or a boy and a girl.

Mirror twins is used to describe a type of individual, or monozygotic twin pairing in which the twins are matched as if they are looking into a mirror with defining characteristics like birthmarks, dominant hands, or other features on opposite sides.

Identical twins are also known as monozygotic twins. They result from the fertilization of a single egg that splits in two. Same genes and DNA. And always of the same sex.

ABOUT THE AUTHOR

56

A lady that has seen ups and downs. Life experiences that could rival those of kings, queens, and Paupers.

A twin that speaks the truth and encourages others to reach new potential.

With hopes and dreams for herself and others, she reaches her everything by hard work and carrying for others as if she was working for herself.

Come and experience this life story with all of us who know and love her as a gifted author who can touch your soul no matter how old or young you are.